THE SINGING HEART
A BOOK OF QUIET REFLECTIONS

A STUDY GUIDE FOR INDIVIDUALS & GROUPS

STUDY GUIDE BY RON DITTHARDT

Original book written by Ivan Ilyin and translated by Alexandra Weber

Orthodox Christian Translation Society

©2017 Orthodox Christian Translations Society
Memphis, Tennessee

The Singing Heart: A Study Guide for Individuals & Groups
Ron Ditthardt

ISBN: 978-0692983188

Cover art: Mariamni Plested, "Russian Scene"

CONTENTS

PUBLISHER'S FOREWORD 5

    About the Author 7
    Foreword 7

STUDY QUESTIONS

I. FIRST GLIMMERS
Without Love (from a letter to my son) 8
About Fairness 8
His Hatred 9
My Guilt 11
About Friendship 12

II. THE SCHOOL OF LIFE
The Soap Bubble 13
Clouds 14
About Deprivation 14
About Health 15
The World's Dust 16
About Generosity 17
In the Early Morning 18
About Age 19

III. THE GIFT OF PRAYER
About Spiritual Blindness 20
The Mountain Lake 21
The Return 22

About Prayer 23
About the World's Sorrow 24
Mountains 26

IV. VISITING
The Contemplative Poet 27
Fire 27
At the Seaside 28
About Suffering 29
About Death (the first letter) 31
About Immortality (the second letter) 33

V. AT THE GATES
God's Fabric 35
A Christmas Letter 35
A Wasted Day 36
About Patience 36
About the Conscience 38
About Optimism 39
About Sincerity 40

EPILOGUE: THE SINGING HEART 41

ABOUT THE ORTHODOX CHRISTIAN TRANSLATION SOCIETY 43

FOREWORD

"Every writer worries about how he will be read. Will his readers understand him? Will they see what he wanted to show them? Will they feel that which his heart has loved? Who will his readers be? So much depends on this… Most importantly, will they experience that desired spiritual meeting with themes distant yet near, for which the author secretly wrote his book?"

So begins Ivan Ilyin's Foreword to *The Singing Heart*, a work that rewards the reader not only with an understanding of what the author means by a heart that sings, but with a taste of that reality in her or his own heart.

But how can one be the careful reader that Ilyin desires for his work, one who grasps the spiritual insights that he shares and avoids what he describes as "mechanics without soul" and "entertainment without responsibility" (p 13).

Although offering instruction in proper readership lies well beyond the scope and intention of the Orthodox Christian Translation Society, we are pleased to offer this study guide as a gateway to a closer, more systematic reading of this enlightening text. Written by a thoughtful Orthodox layperson, the questions in the study guide allow readers, individually or within a group setting, to not only consider details of the text itself but also invite them to interact with Ilyin's words and thoughts. By pondering these questions, readers may engage Ilyin's essays more slowly and deliberately, affording themselves a chance to have the "spiritual meeting" with the book's themes that the author so desired they have.

STUDY QUESTIONS

ABOUT THE AUTHOR
(Pages 9–12)

1. Given what we know about the author's earlier life experiences, is the title of the book surprising, or what we would expect? Support your answer.

2. What can we learn from Ilyin's attitude and perspective on life?

FOREWORD
(Pages 13–16)

3. What, according to Ilyin, does a person need in order to understand this book?

4. How does Ilyin define "true reading," as opposed to "running printed words through the consciousness"?

I. FIRST GLIMMERS

WITHOUT LOVE (Pages 17–21)

1. Do you agree with Ilyin that "modern mankind has entered into a spiritual crisis unprecedented in its depth and scope"? Why or why not?

2. At the end of this excerpt from a letter to his son, Ilyin states, "We cannot live without love …. And how impatiently will I now await your letter confirming this!" If you could write Ilyin a letter, what would you say?

3. Ilyin asserts that "everything great and ingenious that has been created by man was created out of a contemplating and singing heart." Can you give an example of this from human history?

4. According to Ilyin, what led to the religious crisis of his day?

ABOUT FAIRNESS (Pages 21–26)

5. What kinds of life experiences make it difficult for people to communicate and to agree with one another about what is fair?

6. Do you agree that "fairness is the only thing worth discussing"? Why or why not?

Study Questions

7. How should fairness be imagined?

8. Describe the essence of fairness.

9. Where should we not expect to find fairness?

10. What does Ilyin mean by "objective inequality"?

11. How does Ilyin describe "creative fairness"?

12. What does Ilyin consider to be the most important thing in life?

HIS HATRED (Pages 26–31)

13. How does the individual relate to and interact with the universal spiritual realm?

14. How have you been affected by another person's antipathy?

15. Describe the progression from antipathy to hatred.

16. Describe what emanates from a hateful center. What effects does this have?

17. Describe the progression of emotions we may experience when we encounter someone who bears real hatred toward us.

18. What effects does hatred have on the hater? The hated? What steps does Ilyin suggest we take in response to this problem?

19. According to Seraphim of Sarov, what is man's greatest joy?

20. For what purpose is every human soul designed?

21. What inward-looking questions might we ask ourselves if we wish to understand another person's hatred and animosity?

22. List some key guidelines for resolving hatred between individuals.

23. What end goals should we keep in mind during a reconciliation process?

24. What is the first thing we must convey to another person if we wish to overcome his or her hatred?

25. How must we treat our antagonist?

26. How can hatred be healed? Describe the steps in the process.

27. If at some point the relationship between you and an antagonist is transformed, what resulting effects does Ilyin believe will go beyond the two of you?

28. Have you ever experienced healing in a relationship? Does that experience support what Ilyin is saying in this section?

MY GUILT (Pages 31–36)

29. What is required of us if we are to recognize and bear our own guilt?

30. Why do we chase after evidence for self-justification?

31. How does Ilyin describe the common guilt of the world? What does it entail?

32. Why are there no guilty or guiltless people?

33. What do people who know their own guilt try to do?

34. Describe the steps in the process of coming to accept one's own guilt. What questions must you ask?

35. Once we perceive our fault, what must we do?

36. What must we do to earn the right to explore the question of another person's guilt?

37. What positive or negative motives might lead us to explore the question of the guilt of other people?

38. What positive outcome might result from imagining that the other person's guilt is your own?

ABOUT FRIENDSHIP (Pages 36–42)

39. What are some negatives upon which a so-called "friendship" might be based?

40. What are the characteristics of true friendship?

41. How does Ilyin describe the human spirit?

42. How do true friendships begin?

43. Why does the human spirit refuse to accept loneliness?

44. If we were to form true friendships, what might be some positive outcomes for humanity?

45. Is friendship within everyone's grasp?

46. What are the implications of this chapter for you personally? How might you apply it to your own life?

47. Have you experienced what Ilyin describes as "the natural ease of true sacrifice"?

II. THE SCHOOL OF LIFE

THE SOAP BUBBLE (Pages 43–46)

48. What life lessons does Ilyin draw from his illustration of the soap bubble?

49. What potential can be found in even the smallest and most pointless moments of joy or beauty?

50. In place of waiting passively for beauty or joy to appear, what initiative can we take?

51. What therapeutic value do games have?

52. Describe the steps needed to become "obedient to nature."

53. What qualities must we develop before we attempt to create beauty?

54. How might the joyful moments of your life be more fully experienced and cherished?

55. "If an unwonted moment comes upon us and our joy shatters in a fine mist," how should we respond?

CLOUDS (Pages 47–50)

56. What characteristics of clouds make them therapeutic?

57. What life lessons can we learn from clouds?

58. The contemplation of clouds delivers us from what kinds of problems or difficulties?

59. What do the clouds give us? How are they symbolic?

ABOUT DEPRIVATION (Pages 50–53)

60. How does deprivation help us to achieve "objective success" and victory in the battle of life?

61. How can a fear of deprivation lead to spiritual defeat?

62. On what two conditions does the art of overcoming deprivation depend?

63. How did Anthony the Great perceive the Lord God?

64. What wealth does a poor man possess, if he knows how to be rich?

65. Why is it not good to forego deprivation?

66. What benefits, according to Ilyin, do we derive from deprivation? Does your experience support Ilyin's contention?

ABOUT HEALTH (Pages 53–60)

67. Describe how your own "inner Doctor" guides you in life.

68. List some areas in which a person must achieve balance in order to be healthy.

69. According to Ilyin, how has "going against nature" affected modern man?

70. The loss of what ability, in particular, has caused humanity to "go against nature"?

71. How do we tell the difference between "consulting with one's inner Doctor" and simply indulging our own passions and desires?

72. Ilyin writes that "only by submitting to nature can we govern over it." What does it mean for an individual to "submit to nature"?

73. Do you agree with Ilyin's assertion that God sends us ailments so that we can recover from them? Compare this statement to Psalm 103:3 and 2 Corinthians 12:7-9.

74. Why is patience needed if we are to achieve harmony in life?

THE WORLD'S DUST (Pages 60–65)

75. In Ilyin's analogy, what does dust represent?

76. According to Ilyin, what is necessary for happiness on earth?

77. How does one secure one's freedom in the world?

78. What is the great organizational purpose of the world?

79. Can this purpose ever be realized, or will it always be an ongoing process?

80. For what purpose is every human soul designed?

81. To what does Ilyin compare a person's character?

82. What test does Ilyin prescribe for determining whether a thing is good, i.e., worthy of being chosen and preferred?

83. What types of things does Ilyin call the "dust" of life?

84. How can we avoid being inundated by this "dust" in our own lives?

85. What is the essential crisis of the modern world?

Study Questions

ABOUT GENEROSITY (Pages 65–70)

86. In modern life, to what do people assign excessive value?

87. What is "the art of ownership"?

88. Why was Ilyin's grandfather's woodcarving so well liked?

89. Is there a connection between Ilyin's grandfather's violin playing and the title of this book?

90. Why didn't Ilyin's grandfather marry either of the two wealthy brides with whom he was matched?

91. From which two oppressions must a person be free?

92. What must be our master in order for our work to "sing every joy of life and of God's beauty"?

93. Why are possessions given to us?

94. What might a person who idolizes his own wealth fail to notice?

95. What is the result of "trembling over one's wealth"?

96. What is the purpose of having possessions?

97. What is required for a rich man to be considered to have earned his wealth?

IN THE EARLY MORNING (Pages 70–75)

98. Why is the early morning hour so delightful?

99. Why must days be short?

100. According to Ilyin, what is the function of the darkness of night?

101. Where do sensitive and gentle people find relief from the "poisonous dust of the day"?

102. What are the characteristics of night, as contrasted with the day?

103. What positive effects are bestowed on earth by the stars?

104. When can the very breath of God be felt?

Study Questions

ABOUT AGE (Pages 75–80)

105. How is Ilyin's concept of youth related to the title of this book?

106. According to Ilyin, what is the key to true happiness?

107. Why must we seek to become independent of our chronological age, i.e., the number of years we have lived?

108. How might we overcome our chronological age? List three steps.

109. Describe the joys unique to the child, the youth, the adult, the mature, and the elderly.

III. THE GIFT OF PRAYER

ABOUT SPIRITUAL BLINDNESS (PAGES 81–88)

110. Under what conditions will a person who feels envious and neglected find his or her own mediocrity completely unbearable?

111. Why, according to Ilyin, is atheism a religion?

112. What are the results when atheism is viewed as a "new revelation"?

113. To what kinds of deprivation does Ilyin compare militant atheism?

114. What are the correct responses to militant atheism?

115. Why should believers in God be labeled neither as hypocrites nor daydreamers?

116. List a few of the brilliant scientists and inventors who were believers in God. On what grounds did they acknowledge God? Why?

117. In what is true faith always rooted?

Study Questions

118. What analogies does Ilyin use to show that those who criticize faith and religion lack a firm foundation from which to do so?

119. What kinds of enslavement does atheism bring about?

120. Describe places and events in nature or in human culture where the spirit of God breathes.

121. What example from astronomy does Ilyin use to describe life without God?

122. Historically, what have been the results of godlessness?

123. What is the mission of our generation? Is it different from Ilyin's?

THE MOUNTAIN LAKE (Pages 88–90)

124. What does a mountain lake reflect?

125. Describe the journey to a mountain lake. What does the traveler see and feel?

126. What is the reason for the stillness around the mountain lake?

127. To what does Ilyin compare the mountain lake?

THE RETURN (Pages 90–95)

128. Describe some of the things that modern mankind is experiencing.

129. What is the first goal of every child's upbringing?

130. From what is it imperative that we free ourselves?

131. What is the first step toward prayer?

132. What are the best and most exalted things? How can we recognize them?

133. How is a living desire for God born?

134. What is Ilyin's definition of prayer?

135. How is Christian prayer unique?

136. What are the three greatest comforts we derive from experiencing God's love?

137. What two basic requirements of prayer must we observe?

138. What is the main characteristic of true prayer?

139. What is the effect of every fear, misfortune, and spiritual upheaval that we experience in life?

ABOUT PRAYER (Pages 95–102)

140. What is the purest and most effective comfort known to the human spirit?

141. List the benefits of prayer.

142. What is the path that leads to our life's renewal?

143. What is the one thing, according to Ilyin, that we must accurately determine about every aspect of our life?

144. How do we come to understand the purpose and meaning of life?

145. Can the authority of the world deprive one of one's inner freedom?

146. What might bring a person who has never prayed to prayer?

147. What is the most important and precious thing about religion?

148. Why is prayer "the heart's heat"?

149. Describe how true prayer makes one forget oneself. What are some of the effects of such prayer?

150. What does Ilyin believe is the relationship between prayer and actions in our lives and work?

151. List different kinds of prayer.

152. What great freedom does God give us in prayer?

ABOUT THE WORLD'S SORROW (Pages 102–107)

153. According to which basic law of the world do people rise to perfection? From what does contemplation of this law release us?

154. What higher gift is given to man, which other creatures do not share?

155. How can human beings forget their own suffering?

156. How can our spirit ascend and enter into a blessed nearness to God?

157. List the various emotions you experience when considering the sufferings of your neighbor, of other people, and of all created things.

158. What is the result of rising up against God?

159. What is the first and most basic form of love?

160. When is love liberating?

161. Why is suffering necessary?

162. Why must we accept the necessity of suffering?

163. When will the "great and fruitful mystery" be revealed to us?

164. What was the purpose of God becoming man?

165. What is the new path that has been revealed to man?

MOUNTAINS (Pages 107–111)

166. What inspiration does Ilyin obtain from mountains?

167. What compels someone to climb to the top of a mountain?

168. What lessons does Ilyin draw from his experience of mountains?

Study Questions

IV. VISITING

THE CONTEMPLATIVE POET (Pages 113–117)

169. How does the contemplative poet make way for a new spiritual contemplation?

170. What impulse, according to Pushkin, does the inspired poet heed?

171. What makes the artistic creation of a contemplative poet bigger than its author?

172. Why, when we truly hear the song of the contemplative poet, do we tremble in our hearts and rejoice in spirit?

FIRE (Pages 117–122)

173. What does Ilyin see in the fire?

174. What longings and emotions does fire awaken?

175. What human attributes does Ilyin attribute to fire?

176. What did fire teach our ancestors?

177. What does fire symbolize?

178. What is impossible in this life without fire?

179. What other powers does fire have?

180. How does Ilyin demonstrate that every Christian is familiar with the great religious symbolism of fire?

BY THE SEASIDE (Pages 122–126)

181. Of what is the sea a celebration?

182. Describe the sea as Ilyin sees it.

183. What emotions does the sea evoke?

184. What lessons does Ilyin learn from the sea?

185. What unshakable certainty did Ilyin carry in his heart after visiting the seaside?

186. Why was Ilyin's face moist when he awoke at the seaside?

187. For what end does pain and grief prepare us?

ABOUT SUFFERING (Pages 126–136)

188. According to Ilyin, what remembrance brings immediate relief from suffering?

189. How might we learn to suffer?

190. Describe the essence of the human condition, according to Ilyin.

191. Why does suffering come to us so often and so easily?

192. Why do "the best people suffer the most"?

193. What is the "law of existence" to which Ilyin refers?

194. On what earthly tragedy did Dostoevsky shed light?

195. What devastating consequences would fall upon us if mankind were freed from all suffering?

196. Love is first of all a sense of _____ and _____.

197. What gift do we receive from suffering?

198. What virtues would be impossible to achieve without suffering?

199. Describe the transformation that suffering can produce in our lives.

200. According to Ilyin, when and only when will suffering cease?

201. Why should we not fear suffering?

202. What difficult internal battle must we undertake when we are suffering?

203. What does the path of suffering require? To what does it lead?

204. What is the final and highest purpose of suffering?

205. What are some of the proper and improper responses to suffering?

206. Instead of becoming impatient and despondent, what should a suffering person do?

207. What responses signify our surrender to and defeat by suffering?

208. What must we use to counter pain of the flesh?

209. What is one of the highest skills, according to Ilyin? How can it be acquired?

210. What is the proper response to spiritual suffering, in particular?

211. To what can the sacred purpose of spiritual suffering be compared?

212. What should we do when we are in the grips of spiritual apathy?

213. What does Ilyin call the "easy yoke" and a light burden (Matthew 11:30)?

214. What will lay down the faithful path that leads to true joy on earth?

ABOUT DEATH – THE FIRST LETTER (Pages 136–142)

215. Why does Ilyin have the sense that death can be serene, forgiving, even healing?

216. To what does Ilyin compare death?

217. Why does the certain anticipation of death give life its form and moderation?

218. Why is uncertainty about when death will come a blessing?

219. How might the reality of death illuminate a new beginning of life?

220. What reactions do you have to the idea of death?

221. What does the reality of death slowly teach us?

222. How does the shadow of death affect our ability to distinguish between what is valuable and what is worthless?

223. What is instantly born in the face of death?

224. What important life conclusion comes to us when the danger of death has passed?

225. What does the "shadow" of death teach us?

226. What experience is as irrevocable, mysterious and unfathomably complex as death?

227. What might death become for us, if we understand it fully?

ABOUT IMMORTALITY – THE SECOND LETTER (Pages 142–149)

228. What qualities might keep us from "chasing empty and abstract possibilities"?

229. Why is it impossible to prove the immortality of the soul to a skeptic?

230. What analogy does Ilyin use to describe someone who tries to behold the transcendental while relying only on the physical senses?

231. Why is death frightening to us?

232. Why should we neither despise nor reject our body?

233. How does Ilyin describe the world of nature to which the body admits us?

234. What assures us of the existence of spiritual laws?

235. How and when is the spiritual "I" revealed to us?

236. What are we designed to accept and confirm in ourselves?

237. For what end are we predestined?

238. What qualities does the spark of God produce in us?

239. Why would spiritually blind people preach that the spirit does not exist? What do they regard as sacrosanct?

240. Why are we immortal?

241. As he looks back on his life, what does Ilyin recognize as one of his great joys?

242. What awaits Ilyin, and us, in the future?

V. AT THE GATES

GOD'S FABRIC (Pages 151–154)

243. To what did Ilyin's neighbor's father liken people? What lesson can be learned from this analogy?

244. What lessons can be learned from Jesus' robe?

A CHRISTMAS LETTER (Pages 154–156)

245. When is a person truly alone?

246. When does a gardener put a flower into a bouquet? What lessons can be learned from this?

247. What little secret did Ilyin's mother tell him?

A WASTED DAY (Pages 156–159)

248. With what emotions did Ilyin's wasted day begin?

249. How does Ilyin describe life under the direction of "heartless pedants"?

250. Why was Ilyin's day wasted?

251. How do we build a life?

ABOUT PATIENCE (Pages 159–165)

252. What factor do we often underestimate?

253. How should we respond when we reach the low point of our lives?

254. Upon what does the aptitude for spiritual success depend?

255. What is the purpose of temptation?

256. What ability do we need first and foremost?

257. What is the answer to any uprising of natural hedonism?

Study Questions

258. How can our sensual nature be tamed?

259. How does Ilyin define the art of living?

260. What attitudes help to overcomes every joyless impasse in life?

261. What emotion must be fought from the start, if we are to bear difficulties?

262. What craven words should never appear in our soul?

263. What state of mind can make a person capable of base acts?

264. What should a person do to overcome despair?

265. What two approaches to strengthening one's patience does Ilyin recommend?

266. Why is the human world not alone in its suffering?

267. What must we allow suffering to teach us?

268. How does Ilyin define patience?

269. What is the value of studying human history?

270. What is the result of living with patience?

ABOUT THE CONSCIENCE (Pages 165–171)

271. To what does Ilyin liken the conscience?

272. What does the conscience teach a person?

273. In what state of internal schism do we find ourselves?

274. What does the inclination of the Spirit require of us?

275. What will stay with us for the rest of our lives, if we ignore our conscience?

276. What does true healing and unity of soul require?

277. How might a conscience-driven unity of the human soul be formed?

278. List the things that Ilyin does not consider to be an "act of the conscience."

279. What factors need one consider when acting according to one's conscience? What factors should not be considered?

280. What do we receive from God when we act according to the voice of our conscience?

ABOUT OPTIMISM (Pages 171–174)

281. How does Ilyin contrast "spiritually faithful" optimism with "false" optimism?

282. How is true optimism acquired? What is its source?

283. What characterizes false optimism?

284. What do true optimists know? What do they desire? What do they foresee?

285. With what does the true optimist go forth? What does he or she calmly do?

286. How does Ilyin characterize the true optimist?

287. What does the true optimist do when overtaken by fatigue or uncertainty?

ABOUT SINCERITY (Pages 174–180)

288. What are the advantages of loneliness?

289. What does our earthly shell (the body) protect?

290. Why is individuality given to man?

291. What is necessary for a person to be or become sincere?

292. What is the first and most basic rule of individuality?

293. What characterizes sincerity?

294. How does Ilyin describe an insincere church? An insincere family? An insincere government?

295. According to Ilyin, what is modern man's great misfortune?

Study Questions

EPILOGUE
(Pages 181–186)

296. What is the one true joy on earth, which gives a person almost everything?

297. When does the heart sing?

298. How does Ilyin characterize Dante, Petrarch, or Pushkin?

299. Compare and contrast earthly lovesickness with the singing heart.

300. How does the heart acquire the ability to sing? When does true singing begin?

301. What slumbers in the depths of the human heart and must be aroused within it?

302. What is the most wonderful song of all?

303. Which contemplations of nature in Ilyin's childhood caused his heart to sing?

304. At what sight does every human heart bloom and sing?

305. List some occasions when your heart sings.

306. What happens when you heed the voice of your conscience?

307. Of what can we be truly certain regarding the development of this world?

308. What is the true substance of the world?

309. What principles from Ilyin's book *The Singing Heart* might you apply to your current situation?

ABOUT THE ORTHODOX CHRISTIAN TRANSLATION SOCIETY

The Orthodox Christian Translation Society (OCTS), a Pan-Orthodox non-profit organization, is an international publishing house exclusively dedicated to producing translations of Orthodox texts of unsurpassed quality in languages around the world. Since Pentecost, overcoming language barriers has been an essential part of God's work through His saints. OCTS continues the work begun at Pentecost by supporting the translation of Orthodox texts so that people of every tongue can be inspired by the words of our holy fathers and mothers in the faith regardless of their background. OCTS believes in the unique value of translation for the spiritual edification of the Orthodox Church worldwide.

The mission of OCTS begins with highly qualified Orthodox Christian translators who submit their proposals to translate texts that they believe would be of great benefit in the target language. OCTS chooses proposals to fund based on several criteria, including the competence of the translator, the relevance and importance of the text, the achievability of the project, and the marketability of the final publication. The OCTS Advisory Board affirms which projects they believe would be of the most spiritual benefit. OCTS commits to financially support chosen projects from the first draft of translation all the way through the editing, publication, and distribution of the finished project. OCTS raises funds through grants and donations, invests the proceeds from the sale of our publications back into the organization, and hopes to provide a source of reliable, edifying, and relevant translations for generations.